A Wrongful Criminal Conviction

THE FAILURE OF LADY JUSTICE

Anne Boston Parish, RN, CS, MSN
Family Nurse Practitioner

authorHOUSE®

AuthorHouse™
1663 Liberty Drive
Bloomington, IN 47403
www.authorhouse.com
Phone: 1-800-839-8640

Published by AuthorHouse   05/09/2013

ISBN: 978-1-4817-3346-5 (sc)
ISBN: 978-1-4817-3345-8 (hc)
ISBN: 978-1-4817-3344-1 (e)

Library of Congress Control Number: 2013905223

Dedication

● ● ● ● ● ● ● ● ● ● ● ● ●

I carry your heart with me (I carry it in my heart)
—*e. e. Cummings*

*T*his book is dedicated to my beloved late parents, Ward Jr. and Emma C. Boston. They taught me to be forthright, take responsibility for my actions, above all be honest with my intentions, and always to believe in myself.

To my two wonderful English bulldogs, Gracie and Jack. You are the sunshine of my life and my love forever!

Finally, this book is dedicated to persons who have resolved to pursue the truth concerning some situation regarding which they feel they have been judged unfairly. As Winston Churchill said, "Never, never, never give up!"

Introduction

● ● ● ● ● ● ● ● ● ● ● ● ●

Sweet are uses of adversity.—*William Shakespeare*

I *have learned that American beliefs* and traditional teachings seek to avoid life's adversities. Most people would rather avoid a confrontation or an ill-fated consequence than be the end product of a harmful event. In an adverse event, powerful persons may explore ways to attain personal achievement and gain, while their means and their methods destroy an innocent person or persons. In an adverse event, these powerful people study individualistic and idiosyncratic methods to damage and harm the goodness in others. Many times these powerful people employ cohesive power to target, single out, and sacrifice an innocent person in a mean-spirited style.

Such powerful persons pursue this style of adversity to weaken the virtuous character in others, or perhaps to attain personal reward or greater power. In the end, their actions can damage the personal and professional reputation of an innocent person. I hold an opinion much like William Shakespeare, who said this type of adversity is sweet, because it teaches us to sustain our character. When a person is faced with a harmful event, and is able to sustain his or her character, it is a test of that person's resolve, competence, virtue, and courage.

William Shakespeare was England's greatest and most renowned poet and playwright. Shakespeare argued in the play *As You Like It* that adversity is similar to a toad's "ugly and venomous" appearance. Nevertheless, within its skin, the toad may have the poisonous traits of someone who has the power to seek personal gain, while using that power to influence and undermine the goodness in another person. These powerful people may also direct this type of adversity to harm an innocent person.

A toad may be venomous, but much like the toad's skin, adversity causes each of us to find our core integrity, goodness, and beauty that lies within our own foundation of life.

Does adversity cause us to reflect negatively when faced with an unfavorable outcome? Adversity should teach each of us to reflect and pause when faced with difficulty. There is always a silver lining when we face challenge and hardship.

I would agree, much like Shakespeare, that when we overcome difficulties and sorrow, we have discovered a treasure trove of sweetness. This intimate discovery is part of our personal gain and resolve. Much like the beauty of a rainbow, the discovery of its color and its beauty stems from the creation of a wealth of vibrant colors. The sweetness of the rainbow is the aftermath of the storm, and many times from within the darkness of the storm, come the sunshine and brightness of its sweetness.

Shakespeare explored the notion of overcoming challenges. Doing so is a blessing in disguise because the beauty in attaining personal growth and its unique discovery allows adversity to be overcome. Adversity should be viewed not as a curse, but as a sanction. If we view adversity as a test of personal character, we will be judged by our proficiency in overcoming ill-fated consequences and harm that accompany to hardship.

When we overcome adversity, we become better scholars, and when we are able to understand the value in failure, defeat, and loss, we develop an inner core of strength. This inner core will allow us to traverse and overcome most hostile circumstances. As Shakespeare wrote, it is not the ease and comfort that brings out the best in a man, but rather the roughness and suffering that ennoble each of us to be better people.

I now have the wisdom to recognize that some tasks are not easy to accomplish. If they were easy, anyone could do them! It's through endurance that we become stronger and are better able to overcome the hardships that life sends our way. As William Shakespeare said, "Sweet are the uses of adversity."

Chapter 1
Land of Oz

• • • • • • • • • • • • •

Magnanimity—*A noun that means greatness* of mind; that elevation or dignity of soul that encounters danger and trouble with tranquility and firmness, which raises the possessor above revenge, and makes one delight in acts of benevolence, which makes one disdain injustice and meanness, and prompts one to sacrifice personal ease, interest, and safety for the accomplishment of useful and noble objectives.—*Webster's Dictionary*

I have learned that some journeys take you where you least expect to go and sometimes along the way, you may find the resolve you thought you had lost; you just need to start that journey. I have also learned to celebrate my failures, not just my successes. But, one of my life's important learned lessons is that a walk on the beach is a good way to find some of the answers to so many of my unanswered questions. Yet, I still do not fully understand why so many stood by watching my dreams and reputation shattered.

I have been blessed with many things. Yet believe if the key to my success is to increase my failures, then it only makes sense to celebrate my setbacks as well. Yes, you heard right: if someone turns you down, celebrate it! Without failure there is no success!

When is the last time you rewarded yourself for failing? Probably never! I have learned instead of mentally punishing myself for not succeeding, I buy myself a prize and say, "I'm one step closer to success!" I have finally stopped letting failure have a negative hold on my thoughts and emotions.

If failure is a vehicle that I can use to get to success, then courage is the fuel! Courage is a muscle, and like any muscle, you must develop and strengthen it with lots of exercise. As the saying goes: use it or lose it. It's no different with courage. Use and develop your "courage muscle" by looking fear in the eye and taking action despite it. Each time you take action, the courage muscle gets stronger.

When you don't, your courage atrophies, and before you know it, it's gone. But it doesn't have to be that way. All the courage you could ever want or need to achieve every goal you have is already in you, just waiting for you to take action.

I now live in the Land of Oz. Perhaps I should explain. I now live in Coronado, where the famous author L. Frank Baum wrote the celebrated novel *The Wizard of Oz*. According to the cowardly lion, courage means acting in the face of fear, but Dorothy would argue there is no place like home, in a place that my parents and grandparents called home. That is where I have found the courage to write this story.

Chapter 2
Personal Statement

• • • • • • • • • • • •

In the United States there are grave consequences when an airplane falls from the sky; a truck or automobile has a defective part; a patient is the victim of malpractice, a bad drug, or an erroneous lab report. Serious inquiries are made. What went wrong? Was it a systemic breakdown? Can anything be done to correct the problem and prevent it from happening again? What factors need to be prevalent to prevent senseless acts or adversities that harm innocent people of their life, liberty and pursuit of happiness?

> **You gain strength, courage, and confidence by every experience in which you really stop to look fear in the face. ... You must do the thing which you think you cannot do.—*Eleanor Roosevelt***

This book is not a scholarly manuscript; it presents my opinion rather than a testable hypothesis, an integrated review of literature, or a sampling of a population. The limitations of my writing are great; it is not supported by data or research.

I will not rehash here my many letters, appeals, or *pro se* argumentation to the lower courts of the Commonwealth of Virginia, the US Supreme Court Writ of Certiorari, or Marymount

University. My purpose herein is to focus on leaning forward with a positive outcome, and to explore effective ways to cope with the miscarriages of justice. I make no apology for trying to resolve an unsettling tale that has caused me great harm and social injustice.

The price of greatness is responsibility
—*Winston Churchill*

My story is unassuming: On February 3, 2009, I was to begin my day's work, seeing patients in a clinic that I had founded for the medically uninsured, when two Alexandria police officers came to the door. They advised me on that morning that a police report had been taken from a USPS mail carrier regarding an occurrence that was said to have happened day before, an event that involved me. However, it was just being reported on February 3, even though it happened the day before. They told me the accusation was not supported by any evidence, such as the person involved going to the emergency room or hospital, or by calling 911 to report the occurrence. There were no witnesses at the site of the occurrence except a fellow USPS mail carrier two blocks away, and the alleged act was said to have occurred in daylight, in twenty-eight-degree weather, on a busy highway in front of the clinic, where 40,000 cars travel daily.

The preceding afternoon, the day of the occurrence, I witnessed a USPS mail carrier walk away with my mail-ordered Drug Enforcement Administration (DEA) control-free patient medication and clinic mail, rather than putting it in my outside mailbox. I reported this to the USPS's supervisor. I also sent the US Postmaster General in Washington DC an e-mail, but I did not file a police report. My concern was that a USPS mail carrier had walked off with my patient medication and clinic mail. It was not my intention to harm anyone; I just wanted the USPS mail carrier to return my patient medication and clinic mail in the outside mailbox.

I contacted the USPS's supervisor to request that she return the patient medication and the clinic mail to my outside mail box. The supervisor said, "No, you have to pick it up at the post office." This episode began a very expensive chain of court appearances for something I absolutely did not do.

In my fear and concern due to this very serious and alarming accusation, I followed the police officer's direction. I never thought to call my malpractice insurance carrier for legal assistance. I put my trust in the integrity of the Alexandria police officers; a defense attorney that I had retained, and later discovered had been Alexandria's prosecuting attorney for more than a half dozen years; and the Commonwealth's prosecuting attorneys, to do what was right. I trusted that they would know that this tale and a criminal assault and battery charge would have the potential to end my professional career. In my opinion, they did not render the assistance necessary to review this accusation, and to have it successfully dismissed prior to going to court. I also felt there were huge gaps in my defense.

There was nothing to gain from allowing this USPS mail carrier to file a police report that damaged my professional and personal reputation. I never felt the Commonwealth prosecuting attorneys reviewed the allegations or looked at the case for the profound long-term consequences that I would suffer. I also never felt my defense attorneys worked to have this allegation dismissed. In my appeals, which are on the Internet, I was disappointed in the lack of courtroom questions or any supportive evidence to demonstrate the veracity of this tale. In my initial court trial, the judge ruled "two against one" due to a statement from a fellow USPS mail carrier witness, who was two blocks down the street. All of my appeals were denied.

The tragedy of this story is that I put my faith, hope, life, liberty, and pursuit of happiness in the good hands of the Commonwealth of Virginia and my defense attorneys, and to this day I feel they never had my best interest at heart. I also feel it was a conflict of my interest for them to continue to try to have me settle or accept a plea bargain of disorderly conduct. My attorneys had suggested I agree to plead guilty on this lesser charge rather than to the original assault and battery. I would not accept any "guilty as charged" verdict, because to do so would have constituted an admission of an act that I absolutely did not commit. I continued to hope the accusation and conviction would be resolved in my favor, but the courts ruled against me.

Up until that time, I had never been involved in anything like this. In my effort to be patient and to comply with the law, I used my free time to go back to school. I applied to and was accepted into a doctoral program to complete my doctor of nursing practice degree. When I applied for admission, I also applied for national and local scholarship money, which would support the high tuition payments that I was expected to pay. I was granted most of my tuition funds in scholarship money, so I was satisfied that my legal struggles would resolve with a positive outcome, as I had anticipated my doctoral degree would afford me.

One semester prior to being awarded my doctorate, and having cautiously shared my legal struggles with the university, I received a letter that advised me that despite a 3.6 GPA (on a 4.0 scale), I was being dismissed for academic failure.

I still do not know the reasons for my academic dismissal. The university's provost had granted my petition to graduate, and I had never been counseled for academic failures prior to my abrupt academic dismissal. Neither do I understand why a university would allow me to be awarded scholarship funds and then dismiss me, knowing that I would therefore have to pay back all of the $50,000.

I have learned that part of coercive power is to demote or punish a person by an action that has ill-fated consequences. Such action can cause harm to someone's personal or professional progress. I understand that the university gave me false hope, which is the reason I could not see my imminent dismissal. In essence, I was blindsided by false hope due to never being given adequate information or direction by the university faculty and staff. This type of strategy detracted me from seeing coercive power being spent that ultimately resulted in my dismissal and public humiliation.

About the time I was being dismissed, the university's alumni board terminated the board position to which I had been voted by fellow alumni. All the while during this time, I was to receive the highest award the university could present an alumnus, and the following year the city of Alexandria presented me with the highest public health service award that could be awarded to a health care provider from the Alexandria Public Health Advisory Commission.

Every day I feel some of my failures are drawing me closer to my successes. I have accomplished much, and many would say I am a strong woman. But that is no reason to destroy and damage my good name. Eleanor Roosevelt once said, "No one can make you feel inferior but yourself." However, as former President Jimmy Carter said, "Life is not fair." Nevertheless, President John F. Kennedy said it so eloquently, "The courage of life is often a less dramatic spectacle than the courage of a final moment; but it is no less a magnificent mixture of triumph and tragedy. A man does what he must—in spite of personal consequences, in spite of obstacles and dangers and pressures—and that is the basis of all morality."

Chapter 3
Every Family Has a Story

• • • • • • • • • • • • •

Every *family has a story*, and every member's story is worth telling—certainly for the living family, but even more so for upcoming generations. I have learned that experiencing history through the eyes of another person's perspective can offer unexpected insight into your own. I once heard a phrase that goes like this: "I have learned that my past does not define me, it has only prepared me." I would argue that I was not prepared for what I experienced, yet within the course of my life, I have learned to accept what I could not change. Dale Carnegie said it so well, "When we have accepted the worst, we have nothing more to lose. And that automatically means—we have everything to gain.

The Storyteller

I am told that every so often a person comes along who can take a quite ordinary thought and capture the imagination of a memory. Such a person can see a lot of the ordinary in day-to-day pastimes, and note something transformative about it. Then something curious happens, like the flip-flop of inattentiveness to awareness: she experiences a moment of inspiration. She is compelled not only to share an idea, but to tell a story.

Anne Boston Parish, RN, CS, MSN Family Nurse Practitioner

I have been told I am a storyteller. And so with that idea, I will tell my story. I have a tendency to like to talk, to share what I know and what I have learned. I always thought those around me were keenly interested in what I had to say. I realize it has been my biggest downfall, and my one trait that has been most misunderstood by so many.

My story and legacy is a tragic tale of personal loss and professional academic heartbreak. I am the only person who has been harmed by it; no one else suffered any unfortunate consequences, either directly or indirectly, nor did anyone else step up to offer support, defend me, or set the record straight. I am not a master of the law, nor am I an attorney, but I am able to recall the facts of these events, and my writing here presents only my opinion.

Now it's hard for me not to talk about being judged, because being passionate about telling the truth is a big part of who I am. If I get the slightest sense that someone is looking at me curiously, or attempting to figure out whether I actually *did* what I was accused of, I jump on the chance to talk about myself and my family. And as my words flow, I realize the person I am speaking to has no clue what I am talking about, because rather than just asking me plainly whether the legal accusation made against me and court's verdict are true, she has already made up her mind. She has judged me for something I did not do, and I am once again faced with the consequences imposed on me by the Commonwealth of Virginia's courts and the academic setting of Marymount University.

Last February I sold my home in Alexandria, Virginia, after selling the Queen Street Clinic. I left a community that I had been a member of for almost thirty years. I have learned that each new beginning involves a loss of some kind. I said good-bye to my beautiful home and to a community that I loved.

I was to begin a new life. I was thrilled; I was sad, worried, and confused why I was leaving my beloved home and the only community I had known for all these years. I was experiencing something seemingly silly and it provoked the same feelings of unsureness: I was taking a chance on change, filled with a sense of excitement, the promise of something new, and the deep satisfaction of having met a challenge. I began to think this idea was unattainable. I was letting go; I did not know what lay ahead, and it was overwhelming. I was taking a chance on change, and I put my emotional security at risk. Even looking forward to a positive change triggered anxiety that I thought was due to my own inability to meet this self-inflicted personal challenge and expectation. After settlement on my home, I put my two English bulldogs in the car, and with a GPS in place, began my drive out of Virginia, across country, back to my late parents' hometown in California. This was to be a new beginning.

I moved to a small town that my parents and grandparents loved and called home. Perhaps in my mind I missed my parents and longed to be near them, even if that meant living near their gravesite. Life is a mystery. I thought I would feel at home, and I began to look forward to the repair of an old cottage that I purchased in Coronado, but I really began to feel the loss of displacement and change. I moved back to a small town that I had many times visited to see my parents; but now I feel foreign in a town that I used to call home. Sometimes I think the objects of your desire, the things you long for, never happen. It seems life happens when you least expect it. So I journeyed home to be closer to my parents' graves, but soon learned a great deal about myself, my parents, and my family of origin.

Throughout this unpleasant experience in Virginia and its legal ordeal, I had hoped it would not follow me to Coronado, but it did. I discovered that the Internet, while a resourceful tool, has become an open book that shares sordid legal opinions and other negative information about me. As much as I would have liked to feel welcomed and embraced by those who live in Coronado, I have remained detached, and I do not feel a part of a community that I thought would provide me with a second chance.

In a small town that hosts political parties, social gatherings, garden club memberships, book clubs, dance clubs, and committee work, I feel very much on the periphery of life. The tragedy with my legal struggles is so profound that I truly cannot fathom that anyone would believe my story was made up. I was an accomplished family nurse practitioner with an impressive resume, but beaten down by a legal system that damaged my good family name and reputation. The personal pride I felt was justifiably derived from my accomplishments, yet tinted with anxiety and shadowed by loneliness due to such a huge personal and professional loss.

I now know that some people believe anything written on the Internet or Facebook. Toward the end of my legal struggles, and in my desperate effort to get legitimate support, I reached out to the social network Facebook. I soon realized no one was there to help me, nor did anyone respond; I may have just embarrassed myself more than I should have. One life lesson I learned was that the people I thought would come forward and help me undo this embarrassing and difficult ordeal did not reach out to provide any help. Again I faced the isolation of not having a support system.

Nevertheless, I began to pick up cues, both verbal and non-verbal, especially when someone asks me about the veracity of the legal opinion that will forever circulate on the Internet. I really want to say "the courts just got it wrong." But the lesson I have learned is that behind all the closed doors and the secret clubs in Coronado, no matter what I say, people will talk about my past and exclude me from groups. And no kidding—as the title of Thomas Wolfe's novel puts it: you can't go home again. Perhaps Bonnie Prudden understood how time marches on when she wrote, "You can't turn back the clock, but you can wind it up again." Time marches on, and so should the living …

Chapter 4
Throughout my Life

● ● ● ● ● ● ● ● ● ● ● ●

Being defeated is often a temporary condition.
Giving up is what makes it permanent.
—*Marilyn vos Savant*

Through My Eyes

I have been blessed throughout my life. I was born to good and loving parents and reared in a home filled with love, guidance, and empowerment. It took me a long time to learn that I would be even more blessed if I were to mine the riches of my parents' past. My key to this treasure trove came in the form of a personal and professional crisis. But first let me ponder a bit about my parents' generation, which journalist Tom Brokaw dubbed the "greatest generation."

This group was possessed of a superior ethical and work conduct and lived during and was shaped by a unique period of America's history, one that isn't likely to come about again. It was composed of dramatic downs and ups and exacerbated by a frenetically escalating pace of life itself, as amazing inventions began to change the world.

My mom and dad were among those steadfast sentinels of the twentieth century who were children of the Great Depression, that aptly named period of economic and spiritual devastation that battered lives and scorched souls. My parents came of age during World War II, when men were eager to fight for freedom and to move beyond their parents' simple, basic, and humble lifestyles. The "greatest generation" developed a close bond as they banded together to protect America's freedoms, a bond they still share today. Nearly all the able-bodied young men, actually boys for the most part, went off to war in the early 1940s. It was prior to my dad leaving for the Western Pacific that my grandmother Boston had a portrait commissioned of my dad in uniform. Years ago, my parents gave me this charcoal portrait, and even today, it is a portrait that causes me to reflect on an era gone by.

The portrait has hung in my home for years. Alongside the portrait hang the medals my dad earned. His facial expression captures a seventeen-year-old man leaving behind his desire to complete music school, but as all young men did, earning his wings and joining the many men who flew for nearly four years off a carrier in the Western Pacific. My dad flew Hellcats and frequently spoke of his nighttime carrier landings with a third of his squadron not making it back to the carrier. I have to believe, for all the scolding I received, it was secondary to his sacrifices and of those who sacrificed that we as Americans live in a free country. These stories of nighttime carrier landings and the loss of his fellow pilots I heard as a young girl, and I believe they were the foundation of a strong military upbringing filled with honor of country and perfection as a person.

My father used to quote President Franklin Delano Roosevelt:

"You have nothing to fear, but fear itself." Those words of comfort have stuck with me, because I really have reason to fear. No one came forward to recant their tales as only human error. I would suspect they felt to do so would be an admission of guilt. But I have learned that not only is wisdom wasted on the young, it is acquired in threefold ways as Confucius said: "First by reflection, which is the noblest; second by intention, which is the easiest; and third by experience, which is the bittersweet."

Chapter 5
A Strong Woman

• • • • • • • • • • • •

I*have been told I am* a strong woman, one who commands a strong personality, and that I am uncompromising, outspoken, and too candid, but honest, loyal, kind, and very generous. I am also the firstborn child and only daughter born into a military family. I survived a strict military upbringing with parents who demanded, expected, and settled for no less than excellence and perfection in everything that I did.

All the same I have learned that in life there are two kinds of people, ones who build you up, and ones who tear you down. In light of my learned experience, I just need to thank them both because I would argue both experiences have equal value, especially if there are lessons to be learned that will benefit those who come after me.

As an avid reader, I found in Doris Kearns Goodwin's historical chronicle *No Ordinary Time* that Eleanor Roosevelt's description of her feelings about her father was similar to what I felt about my father. It was Eleanor's father who "acquainted Eleanor with grief, and he gave her the ideals that she tried to live up to all her life by presenting her with the picture of what he wanted her to be—noble, studious, religious, loving and good."

Goodwin continues to describe Eleanor as a person who willed herself to become the accomplished daughter her father had decreed her to be, the fearless woman that would make him proud. Every inch of her journey was filled with peril and anxiety, but she never stopped moving forward. Goodwin cites that Eleanor always was to remember, "You must do the thing you think you cannot do." I grew up with this notion of respecting and fearing my father and always being guided by authority.

On occasion I have been told I live in a dream world, most likely due to my love of books. I learned at an early age that a book allows me to travel to far-off places and to discover the different pathways to becoming an accomplished daughter. Becoming an accomplished daughter was something I learned early in my life. I learned from my mistakes that I needed to gather my strength to overcome all obstacles courageously to satisfy my parent's expectations of me. As a young girl, I used to hide books under my mattress so I could wake up in the middle of the night to read them. Later in life, when I visited my parents, my father shared with me that when he couldn't sleep, he too would read in the middle of the night. Much like my father's is my love for books.

Strong women are frightening to many people, and to those in positions of authority, they can be daunting. I often wonder: were a man equally as strong, would it be as intimidating? I must admit I lost much of my intensity in the course of a three-year legal battle, the death of my father, and the following year, the death of my mother. I sank to an all-time low: I had lost a court battle; lost both of my parents; had one semester to complete to be awarded my doctorate; and without cause was dismissed from school.

Much like Eleanor Roosevelt, I learned to understand that promises were made to be broken, and that no one's love for me was meant to last. I must admit, I have read about Winston Churchill and the dark dog of depression that plagued him, but Goodwin's description of Eleanor's melancholy was similar to my feeling of sadness and despair, and to my great disappointment in the indifference of those who stood by and shattered my dreams and reputation. I once read a statement, who wrote, "With women, it's all about confidence and helping them believe that they can do whatever they want to do, and they don't have to change themselves in order to be successful. Just be mindful, there may be those who are watching and waiting to destroy a strong woman."

Most strong women are not aware of their effects on men and other women. They usually don't understand why both genders seem to have a hard time with them. Women who are successful in their own fields usually command strong personalities, are assertive and persuasive, have a strong need to get things done, and are willing to take risks. I am often told I am intense. I don't regard this as a compliment, but it's a phrase often used to describe me. Strong women know what they want, and they are usually perceptive, always viewing things from an angle that's different from the way others seem them.

One problem that a strong woman may have is not being aware of her adversaries. So why do women who possess strong personalities many times not get what they want? Or why do their adversaries find ways to harm them? Because strong women are viewed as threats. They don't pass up opportunities they believe in. They say what they feel, and mean what they say. They don't conform to norms that society dictates, only those that are acceptable to their morals.

One difference in personality styles between a woman who is strong and one who is not is the stronger woman's ability to read situations with accuracy and take in information from all sides. A strong woman has the willingness and the vision to see that all sides of a situation enhance her persuasive ability. She doesn't give up when the going gets tough; has good listening skills to illicit more than one opinion; but really listens to learn, reflect, and then implement a plan that incorporates the best of everyone's ideas. Women of this personality type do not have many friends, despite their commanding personalities and their interest in listening to people. They are seldom included in groups unless they are the leader or speaker. I have learned that you just have to get to know a strong woman before concluding that you cannot get along with her.

Sometimes strong women are targeted as troublemakers, as ones who are always looking at putting a square plug into a round hole. But just because someone has a strong personality is no reason to harm her. Because I have a strong personality, my writing relates acts intended to harm me deliberately. I remember two conversations with my attorneys. On one occasion they asked, "Why do you think you are so important?" On another they told me, "Stop telling everyone how great you are." Those words reflected that they misunderstood the concept behind my clinic's mission. I never referred to myself, only to the work that I did for medically uninsured patients in my primary care family practice clinic as contrasted with what happens in an emergency room.

A Wrongful Criminal Conviction

I have learned that anyone can be convicted of an act that they did not do because of problems that plague many criminal proceedings. For me, my conviction was due in part to the disdain so many felt for me and for my strong personality, also having already been labeled a strong and difficult woman determined to, at all expense, provide medical care to those less fortunate without medical insurance. Or my conviction may have been the consequence of inept defense lawyers, overzealous prosecutors, coercive interrogation tactics, and unreliable statements made in court by a witness who was not at the clinic, but two blocks down the street.

I now recognize that most wrongful convictions result from at least one of three common predisposing circumstances. One, the authorities seek to get a conviction. Two, the accused is a marginalized outsider. Three, the evidence is unreliable. In my case all three circumstances were present, which allowed the police to make mistakes that are commonly found in convictions, but many times never addressed prior to the court appearance.

My conviction changed my life, my life was damaged on a number of levels, and my reputation effectively ruined. Presently, I seek only to learn the reasons for my academic dismissal, and to receive an absolute pardon by the governor of the Commonwealth of Virginia. I want only to achieve closure and peace. For me, closure implies an end to something. I am trying to find the answers that will close the unresolved questions around the issues in an accusation, conviction, and academic dismissal. The problem with finally having the unanswered questions resolved, I would argue, is that having answers to these questions will not return the lost time or expense, nor negate the effect this has had on me personally;

but the resolution will teach me strategies with which I might help others avoid being convicted. To the end, only if this book is read, and read and read by those who not only hold the keys to the kingdom, but read by those who believe making up a tale has no negative consequence on an innocent person.

Therefore, some would argue it would better to destroy a strong woman or just put her in her place, than tolerate her presence or success. I would argue that being a strong woman starts with pulling together a group of people who may have nothing in common and getting them to buy into a vision of themselves as a collective group who can achieve uncommon results to correct at least some small part of prevailing social injustice.

Alexandria is a small town community that sits behind struggling police and politicians who appear to find glory served by destroying the hopes and dreams of one woman. That woman is me, and I did nothing more than to successfully provide family practice in a health care facility, the whole purpose of which was to serve the medically underserved.

Chapter 6
Do Not Judge Me

• • • • • • • • • • • • •

There are people who judge you without having all the facts, supporting data or evidence. I once heard a phrase that goes like this, "Do not judge me until you know me, do not underestimate me until you have challenged me, and do not talk about me until you have talked to me."

I am the firstborn daughter of a military family. I survived a strict military upbringing with parents that demanded, expected, and settled for no less than excellence and perfection in everything that I did. There was never any room for failure. Hence I believed I was capable of doing anything that was legally and academically attainable.

I have learned there is no perfect parent–child relationship. My relationship with my mom and dad was no different from that of any other daughter in a military family. I was raised in a loving home with strict parents that taught me, "Be forthright, take responsibility for your actions, above all be honest with your intentions, and always believe in yourself." My parents frequently said to me that I was a strong young lady, made with a purpose, and that I commanded a strong personality. My mom would often compare me to my Grandmother Boston, my mother's mother; Nanny; my Aunt Caroline; and my Aunt Mary, all strong, driven women ahead of their time.

At an early age I learned the meaning of empowerment. My father was an attorney, and my mom did not question his authority, so I learned not to question him or anyone in authority. As I have often said, "The power players hold the keys to the kingdom." One gift my parents bestowed to me was their unconditional belief and trust in my ability to make a difference in the world; they believed that anything was possible. They always said, "Everything is attainable; you just have to work to earn it, never sitting on your laurels." My dad once made a reference to me as another "Saint Theresa." What a kind complement!

I recall my brother telling a story that our dad didn't think he (my brother) should take a vacation because when he came back, he might not have had a job. My dad had great vision and insight; though I think at the time I was just too young to appreciate his strengths. The funny part of my brother's story is that I did take a vacation—and upon my return I was fired. Go figure.

I learned from my parents the ideals of integrity, honesty, and loyalty. My parents had each other, and for their sixty-one years of marriage, each devoted every day to the other spouse. I saw the integrity of my father and the loyalty of my mom as being the norm in their world. But I learned this norm was not to be the same in a cruel world, which I was soon to learn lives by bias, prejudice, and dishonesty.

My mom taught me many things. When I stumble, this one thing always comes to mind: Some people think the idiom "to fall from grace" means to lose status, respect, or prestige. I would rather believe that no one falls from grace. One may stumble, but faith gives one perspective, focus, and determination to not give up.

How you climb up the mountain is just as important as how you come down the mountain. And so it is with life, which for many becomes one gigantic test followed by one gigantic lesson. In the end, it all comes down to one word: grace. It's how you learn to accept winning and losing, good luck and bad luck, the darkness and the light. I would prefer to think of it as saving grace.

Chapter 7
Adversity is Human

• • • • • • • • • • • • •

Adversity humanizes our life and those around us.
—*Author unknown*

Each of us has experienced moments of hardship. These hardships help us learn lessons of greatness. They assist us to become keenly focused on the world of misfortune. Hardships have become the real test of character. Anyone who faces a hardship or a time of difficulty comes out a better person—one who is more confident about facing the challenges of the world.

Hardships and difficulties are the ladders on which we climb to success. Nothing great can be achieved, or has ever been achieved, without grappling with difficulties. All the great men of the world are those who faced difficulties bravely and then overcame them. Those who lead a life of ease and comfort can never achieve much. Nothing is to be expected of such people, but everything is possible for those who have faced difficulties and have failed but have persisted in spite of failure.

Is Misfortune a Blessing in Disguise?

Man's life course is never smooth. Life is definitely punctuated with ups and downs. Hunger, disease, disappointment, frustration, poverty, and misery—all these form an essential part of man's life. These situations prove perilous in cases of those who do not have courage and endurance. But those who cope with them with fortitude, resourcefulness, and heroic spirit equip themselves with extraordinary virtues that ensure success after success in future life.

**The heroes of strife are those who struggle against
the spells of misfortune.—Author unknown**

Adversities are experiences that remove veils of delusion from our eyes. Adversity is the acid test of friendship because it unmasks friends and exposes rivals. Adversity also helps to reveal the depth of love of family members. Adversity makes you understand unequivocally how kith and kin and near and dear can turn their faces against you in darkness and in sorrow. Thus the realities of the world speak to you, and you taste firsthand a varied experience of worldly behavior from within your immediate family and from those you may call your circle of friends.

Adversity may just be an opportunity to keep us awake, active, alert and ready to cope with any situation that arises. Difficulties vanish when you face them boldly. Opportunities to do so should be welcomed because they test one's resolve and provide chances to reap a rich harvest of experiences. Adversities should be considered occasions to impart valuable training experiences. Thus adversity is never a curse, but a blessing in disguise.

Adversities are like thieves that take to their heels at the first encounter. What appears to be a mountain you're not sure you can climb is scaled in a bold attempt, and paths previously unseen open out to view. Everest was conquered by those who boldly faced the dangers in their way and did not falter in their attempts, in spite of initial failures. Columbus discovered the Americas because he faced the unknown wild oceans with confidence and courage and did not allow anticipated difficulties to stop him. All of human civilization is a record of the exploits of those heroic souls who were undeterred by difficulties that got in their way. To them difficulties were like spurs that goaded them on to make yet greater efforts.

Chapter 8
A Hard Schoolmaster

• • • • • • • • • • • •

*S*tudents are afraid of a hard schoolmaster. A hard teacher gives homework to students and then disciplines them if they do not perform. Usually, the hard schoolmaster has the good of the students at heart. The teacher can make student's career; and years later, is often that one schoolmaster that a successful person will refer to as his mentor. Difficulties are also good for man in the long run, so one should not be afraid of them.

Difficulties train and develop a person's natural faculties. Just as herbs give out their sweet fragrance when they are crushed, so a man of real ability or virtue shines all the brighter when pressed with difficulties. So we should not be afraid of difficulties; rather we should welcome them. They are like the bitter pills the doctor gives his patient to cure him. Adversity is for our own good. It may be bitter at the time, but its uses are really sweet.

The English philosopher, lawyer, and scientist Francis Bacon believed people should fight bravely against all sorts of unfavorable circumstances that affect each of us, and that fortitude is the virtue of adversity. Bacon believed that we should not tamely or calmly accept negative outcomes or adversity that dictates the coercion of circumstances. He believed that sometimes, "It would appear that Fate constantly conspires against us." Do waves of misfortune keep people continuously engaged in the struggle against each other? It is not that Nature is a sadist; but in its own mysterious way, Nature places obstacles in our way to test our courage, patience, and character.

There is nothing like the emptiness in the presence of a natural disaster. The consequences of an earthquake, flood, or drought are always a mixed blessing. They bring along with them new hopes, openings, or new perspectives for an outlook or early spring thaw. Adversity shakes us, but it also unfolds before us opportunities to face the stresses and strains, and to emerge victorious with the help of our internal courage and resourcefulness. For example, a war may take a toll of millions of lives and cause massive destruction. But wars bring some good as well. Industries reap financial benefits from war. Also, war reduces unemployment, and war makes the nation stand united.

When Americans are faced with senseless acts of violence, our hearts ache for those who have been harmed. These actions bring together a frail society longing for reasons to help them better understand the basis for them. These events unite a country with a cause that evokes outrage and distain for the loss of lives, massacres, and wounds that may never heal.

Defeat and Failure

Not everyone's expectations in life are fulfilled. Even great people experience failure because everyone fails at least once in a lifetime. Part of the difference between regular people and great people may be seen in how some great people handle defeat, failure, and loss. Great people learn to use life's lessons to adjust their experiences with those around them. These lessons are priceless, and if applied will help enable effective communication and decrease confrontation.

There are many who would argue I am not a great person. But I have learned to handle defeat with courage, dignity, and kindness. Great people find answers to questions about failure and are able to achieve closure. Sometimes the answers are not what great people want to hear, but great people seek answers to attain closure. While others give up, great people think of ways to resolve their adversities.

Chapter 9
Bystander Effect

● ● ● ● ● ● ● ● ● ● ● ●

**Wrong does not cease to be wrong because
the majority share in it.—*Leo Tolstoy***

The Bystander Effect is often seen in organizations or businesses where people see behavior that is unacceptable, unsafe, illegal, or even criminal, and do not report its presence, even when they are affected by this behavior. I write about the Bystander Effect because it directly affected me. In my readings, I learned about this process, and felt it would be appropriate to incorporate into this book. I'm not an expert in this area of human behavior, and only use it as one supportive aspect of my trial.

I felt disappointed by the indifference of those who shattered my dreams and my reputation, but on a different plane, with persons who stood by and watched me descend into a cavernous pit with no support to catch me when I hit rock bottom. I saw this indifference at different levels throughout the Commonwealth of Virginia Courts and at Marymount University. I felt no one truthfully looked at the long-term damage I would experience if I were prosecuted and convicted of this made-up tale. I will never understand how the Commonwealth of Virginia could look at my past accomplishments, and with no cause to believe the story, or any evidence to support it, prosecute me.

At the same time, the mayor of Alexandria, Virginia was to give me the highest award that could be received by an individual or group by the Alexandria Public Health Advisory Commission, but did not fully recognize the damage that I would experience as a result of the prosecution.

Many people do not want to take action when they see unacceptable behavior, and some of them see nothing unreasonable about their inaction, even if it harms another person. Perhaps some of them, even though they know someone is being harmed, fear something unpleasant will happen to *them*. This fear is often shared as being the primary reason they do not report an incident or step up to defend the person being harmed.

This type of adversity, the Bystander Effect, is psychologically a determinant to anyone who is targeted. In many organizations, the Bystander Effect is viewed as an opportunity to stay alert, awake, and committed; but how many observers fail to step up and report improper or illegal behavior? Or worse, these same people feel they comprise their ethical and work standards to go along with everyone else?

The psychological and long-term outcomes are profound for an innocent person who is allowed to be used as a target or pawn, or to be harmed. The worst outcome is that colleagues or superiors do not report unacceptable, unsafe and illegal behavior, but allow it to be promoted and consistently overlooked by groups of people unwilling to report its presence.

Research regarding the Bystander Effect reveals a wide variety of organizations have implemented procedures to correct injustice when innocent people are harmed. This process has begun to strengthen the fairness of formal decision-making; the quality of treatment received by all persons; and the fairness of decision-making by more than one person.

Persons interviewed gave these reasons for not speaking up:

- Fear of retaliation, or other losses
- Bad consequences for them or reprisal
- Being bullied
- Being made an example of
- It is better to ignore
- It is important to keep a low profile
- Fear of becoming responsible for the problem
- Possible loss of professional image or job
- Formidable dislike of formal investigations
- Not getting a tenured position
- Thinking someone else would speak up
- No one cares what I think
- I do not want to get involved; my family member will not let me get involved
- It is not the popular thing to do

Chapter 10
Thirty Clever Words to Exercise
in Your Vocabulary

• • • • • • • • • • • • • •

Seven characteristics distinguish the wise: he does not speak in the presence of one wiser than himself, does not interrupt, is not hasty to answer, asks and answers the point, talks about first things first and about last things last, admits when he does not know, and acknowledges the truth.—*Talmud*

This chapter outlines thirty clever words to exercise in your vocabulary and a simple application of the word, when faced with adversity. I now have a better appreciation of how to apply the meaning of each word, and a better understanding of how each word would have helped me overcome some of my adversity. I really believed, and still do, that if you have the facts on your side you will always have the law on your side. This was something my father taught me. But in my case, it did not hold true. I now believe, had I been more insightful, maybe less trusting, and more astute with monitoring the clues that I ignored, I would not have experienced my failures both in the courtroom and academic arena. My life continues to be filled with opportunities, and I am grateful for my unyielding ability to keep my spirits up. It may be a testimony to my strength or just being too stubborn to give up.

1: Smarter

Always make those in authority believe they are smarter than you. Hide your talent and brains. Because you are no longer a threat, everyone will like you.

2: New friendship

Be cautious of anyone who calls you their new friend. Actions speak louder than words. Watch the actions of a new friend. Don't turn your back on a new friend, until that person demonstrates behavior that proves that you can trust him.

3: Business

Keep your business to yourself. Do not share your business with anyone; the less spoken, the better. The more you say, the more likely you are to say something foolish.

4: Character

Your character is the cornerstone of your good name. Be alert to potential negative name-calling or any reference to your good name.

5: Appearance

Everything is judged by its appearance; what is seen as unseen counts for everything. Always look understated. Glamour is never seen as strength unless you are a paid model.

6: Others

Use the wisdom, knowledge, and groundwork of others to further your own work. Never do for yourself what others can do for you.

7: Argue

There is never any short-lived triumph to be gained through an argument. Always agree, even if you know you are right.

8: Unhappy

You can smother in someone else's misery. Associate with people who are happy and fortunate.

9: Enthusiasm

Never show any enthusiasm, especially when you are working. No one likes a happy person, especially someone who likes to come to work.

10: Honesty

One honest move will cover over dozens of dishonest ones. It is better to be honest. Even telling a white lie can defuse an open disagreement.

11: Favor

If you need to ask for a favor, that is okay; just don't remind the person you are calling in a favor. Nothing is gained with a friendly reminder of repaying a favor.

12: Defeat

Never defeat anyone, unless you running for president of the United States or have money machine backing you.

13: Presence

Too much presence makes your appearance less admired. Sometimes being absent is a good thing. Your value becomes more worthwhile.

14: Unpredictable

People are creatures of habit with an insatiable need to see familiarity in other people's actions. Change your habits every day.

15: Offend

There are many different kinds of people in the world, and you can never assume that everyone will react to your strategies in the same way. Never offend or deceive the wrong person or a person in authority.

16: Commitment

It is a fool who always rushes to take sides. Do not commit to any side or cause but your own side.

17: Recreate

Do not accept the roles that society imposes on you. Recreate yourself by forging a new identity, one that commands attention. Be the master of your own image rather than letting others define it for you.

18: End

The ending is everything. Plan all the way to it, taking into account all the possible consequences, obstacles, and twists of fortune that might reverse your hard work and give the glory to others. By planning to the end, you will not be overwhelmed by circumstances, and you will know when to stop.

19: Accomplishments

Your actions must seem to be natural and executed with ease. All the toil and practice that go into them, and also all the clever tricks, must be concealed. When you act, act effortlessly, as if you could do much more. Avoid the temptation of revealing how hard you work – it only raises questions. Teach no one your tricks or they will be used against you.

20: Dreams

People often avoid the truth when it is ugly and unpleasant. Never appeal to truth and reality unless you are prepared for the anger that comes from disenchantment. Life is so harsh and distressing that people who can manufacture romance or conjure up fantasy are like oases in the desert: Everyone flocks to them. There is great power in tapping into the fantasies of the masses.

21: Weakness

Everyone has a weakness. This weakness is usually insecurity, an uncontrollable emotion or need; it can also be a small secret pleasure. Either way, once found, it is a thumbscrew you can turn to your advantage.

22: Timing

Never seem to be in a hurry. Hurrying betrays a lack of control over you, and over time. Always seem patient, as if you know that everything will come to you eventually. Become a detective of the right moment; sniff out the spirit of the times, the trends that will carry you to power. Learn to stand back when the time is not yet ripe, and to strike fiercely when it has reached fruition.

23: Think

If you make a show of going against the times, flaunting your unconventional ideas and unorthodox ways, people will think that you just want attention and that you look down upon them. They will find a way to punish you for making them feel inferior. It is far safer to blend in and nurture the common touch. Share your originality only with tolerant friends and those who are sure to appreciate your uniqueness.

24: Free

What is offered for free is dangerous. It usually involves either a trick or a hidden obligation. What has worth is worth paying for. By paying your own way you stay clear of gratitude, guilt, and deceit. It is also often wise to pay the full price. There are no cutting corners with excellence. Be lavish with your money and keep it circulating, for generosity is a sign and a magnet for power.

25: Shoes

What happens first always appears better and more original than what comes afterward. If you have a famous parent, you will have to accomplish double his achievements to outshine him. Do not get lost in his shadow or stuck in a past not of your own making. Establish your own name and identity by changing course. Slay the overbearing father, disparage his legacy, and gain power by shining in your own way.

26: Change

Everyone understands the need for change in principle, but in practice people are creatures of habit. Too much innovation is traumatic and will lead to dislike. If you are new to a position of power, or an outsider trying to build a power base, make a show of respecting the old way of doing things. If change is necessary, make it feel like a conscious decision, not just your change.

27: Perfect

Appearing better than others is always dangerous, but most dangerous of all is to appear to have no faults or weaknesses. Envy creates silent enemies. It is smart to occasionally display defects and admit to harmless vices in order to deflect envy and appear more human and approachable. Only gods and the dead can seem perfect with impunity.

28: Achieve

The moment of victory is often the moment of greatest peril. In the heat of victory, arrogance and overconfidence can push you past the goal you had aimed for, and by going too far, you make more enemies than you defeat. Do not allow success to go to your head. There is no substitute for strategy and careful planning. Set a goal, and when you reach it, stop.

29: Definition

By taking a shape, by having a visible plan, you open yourself to attack. Keep yourself adaptable and on the move. Accept the fact that nothing is certain and no lesson is fixed. The best way to protect yourself is to be as fluid and formless as water; never bet on stability or lasting order. Everything changes.

30: Feeling

If you get that sick feeling in the bottom of your stomach or knot in the back of your throat, you probably are in some kind of trouble.

Chapter 11
Purposeful Lessons from Great People

● ● ● ● ● ● ● ● ● ● ● ●

Persons who become the object of harm or adversity deliberately directed at them need to learn a few practical lessons to overcome it. If they don't, the trouble may harm them and others, too.

Getting angry with another person is like throwing hot coals with bare hands: both people get burned.
—Buddha

If you stumble, find constructive ways to seek out the reasons for your defeat, loss, or failure. Simply stated, with the answers in the palm of your hand, you will be able to attain closure, and be at peace. Henry Ford simply stated, "Failure is only the opportunity to begin again more intelligently."

1. Anger is secondary to adversity and covers up hurt and pain. It is the most powerful protection against being vulnerable. It is much easier to get angry again than to feel the hurt. Look beyond the anger and you may uncover fear, insecurity, vulnerabilities, pain, and someone who is searching for power and control due to having his or her

choices removed. When their choices are removed, people lash out and may harm themselves or others.

2. Know the lessons to be learned. When you know them, it keeps you in the game and decreases your chance of defeat, failure, or loss.

3. Know the second chance lessons. These lessons give you real hope, not false hope.

4. Understand adversity expands your knowledge and experience and teases out the significant events of life from the banter.

5. Believe that adversity is equally as significant when harmony. To have a balance when faced with adversity is to attain calmness and peace.

6. Appreciate that adversity is a guide that unmasks our eyes, enabling us to distinguish between the real and the unreal.

7. Trust that adversity instills in each of us the ability to either fix the hardship or make it go away.

8. Remain polite when you are wronged. It is easy to treat people well when they treat you well. The real test is when they treat you badly.

9. Know that there are no failures. Only through failure do we achieve success. Recognize defeat and failure as positive variables in life.

10. Make lemonade from lemons.

Chapter 12
The Meaning of Adversity

• • • • • • • • • • • •

**Life is not about waiting for the storm to pass;
it is about the lesson we learn when we
make it through the storm.**
—*Author unknown*

*A*dversity has different meanings to different people; at the most basic level, adversity is that bad feeling at the pit of your stomach, knowing that no good will ever come of this mess, or simply waking up one day and realizing everyone was playing with a different set of cards.

Adversity comes in different shapes, sizes, colors, and flavors. In my case, adversity became very personal. For someone else it could mean war, hunger, or a violent act that harms others.

Adversity to some may mean:

1.   Disappointment or defeat when not awarded a prize;

2.   Failure when not able to complete a task;

3.   Dismissal from an academic setting;

4. Loss of a loved one;

5. Termination of employment;

6. Rejection by one person or a group of people;

7. That hopeless feeling when a realistic expectation is not attained;

8. False hope;

9. Being blindsided due to having too much trust in those around you;

10. Internal or external threats or events that may be specific to one person, or something similar to a canceled airline flight;

11. A senseless act of violence;

12. A made-up tale that has harmed your personal and professional reputation; or

13. Trusting too much.

One difference between great people and regular people is the great ones' foundation of learned coping and endurance skills. Overcoming adversity begins with courage, kindness, dignity, and sincerity. Even so, overcoming adversity does not begin with anger, because anger can lead to

1. A senseless act of violence;

2. harm to another person;

3. Name calling;

4. Harm directed to others in their personal or professional venues;

5. Hurting the feelings of another person; and

6. Cohesive acts of bullying by persons in positions of power.

Chapter 13
Focus

• • • • • • • • • • • •

**After a defeat, loss or failure, don't find fault.
Find a remedy.**

**Even a mistake may turn out to be the one thing
necessary to a worthwhile achievement.—*Henry Ford***

Become focused when faced with defeat, loss, or failure. When faced with adversity, such as harm, defeat, failure, or loss, begin by getting centered. Focus or pause to reflect on a path of recovery.

- *Pause* – You rarely get in trouble for what you don't say or do. Give yourself the gift of time, even just a few seconds.

- *Compassion for yourself* – Allow yourself a moment of feeling "Ouch, that hurts, I wish this hadn't happened." A neurologically savvy trick for activating self-compassion is to first recall the feeling of being with someone who cares about you. Learn not to beat yourself up.

- *Get on your own side* – This means being for yourself, not against others. It can help to remember a time when you felt strong, such as when you were doing something that was physically challenging, or sticking up for someone you loved.

- *Make a plan* – Start figuring out what you're going to do, or at least where you'll start. After you are on firmer ground, try some logical suggestions to sort through the adversity.

- *Clarify the facts* – What actually happened?

- *Rate the bad event* – Estimate it on a 0–10 scale of awfulness.

- *See the big picture* – Recognize the okay aspects of the situation mixed up with the bad ones. Put the situation in the larger context of unrelated good things happening for you, and your life as a whole. See the biggest picture of all: how your experiences are continually changing, and why it's not worth getting all caught up in them.

- *Reflection* – Consider the causes. Be careful about assuming what happened was intentional. Much of the time you're just a bit player in other people's dramas.

Chapter 14
A Wrongful Conviction

• • • • • • • • • • • •

We shine when we have the courage … to take the first step.

Nearly all men can stand adversity, but if you want to test a man's character, give him power.
—*Abraham Lincoln*

You can agree with me or you can get it wrong.
—*Author unknown*

Being charged with and then convicted of a crime has immediate and severe personal implications for the one accused. It results in a court appearance and can create disdain from friends and even from family members.

A conviction often results in the one convicted being unable to provide for himself. And depending upon the nature of conviction, it means that person may need to retain a skilled attorney or learn how to deal with a lawyer whose eyes are focused on a plea bargain. A conviction can produce the terrible psychological and emotional toll of facing a judge who, in my case, had already assumed guilt.

Without a good lawyer, an accusation almost always leads to a conviction. Conviction results in a criminal record and probation or imprisonment.

The post-conviction struggle for complete exoneration or a judicial declaration of conviction requires a Herculean effort. Appellate courts are not receptive to ordinary claims of police-fabricated evidence, prosecutorial misconduct, faulty forensic evidence, illegal searches and seizures, coercive or involuntary confessions, highly improper lineup procedures, or claims of ineffective assistance of defense counsel. Courts do not recognize "freestanding actual innocence" claims in post-conviction habeas corpus proceedings. Claims of actual innocence must be anchored to a specific constitutional violation and many times take years and years to be fully exonerated for a wrongful conviction.

Chapter 15
Trust

● ● ● ● ● ● ● ● ● ● ● ●

Justice is truth in action.—*Joseph Joubert*

Justice has nothing to do with expediency. It has nothing to do with any temporary standard whatever. It is rooted and grounded in the fundamental instincts of humanity.—*Woodrow Wilson*

**An eye for an eye makes the whole world blind.
—*Ghandi***

An accusation, a conviction, and an academic dismissal can erode one's trust. Bad choices that are based on trust can have negative consequences. In a perfect world, trust has both emotional and logical components. Emotionally, trust is where you expose your vulnerabilities to people, believing they will not take advantage of your openness. Logically, trust is where you have assessed the probabilities of gain and loss, calculating expected utility based on hard performance data, and concluded that the person in question will behave in a predictable manner.

In practice, trust is a bit of both. I trust you because I have experienced your trustworthiness and because I have faith in human nature. When we feel trust, we feel emotions associated with companionship, friendship, love, agreement, relaxation, and comfort.

Justice cannot be one side alone, but must be for both.
—*Eleanor Roosevelt*

Chapter 16
Defeat

● ● ● ● ● ● ● ● ● ● ●

**Defeat should never be a source of discouragement
but rather a fresh stimulus.—*Robert South***

*V*iewing defeat positively is not always easy to do, but it is one of the most common things that great people cite when asked about how they got to where they are. They all say they see defeat as a positive.

When you see defeats as positive, you open yourself up to admitting that you still have a lot to learn. They won't drag you down, and you will move on from the events to bigger and brighter futures.

See defeat as inevitable

**It is inevitable that some defeat will enter even the most
victorious life. The human spirit is never finished when it is
defeated ... it is finished when it surrenders.
—*Ben Stein***

The next thing you need to do is realize that no matter who you are, what industry you are in, and how good you are at what you do, you are always going to experience some defeats. It might not happen every day, but it will happen. No one in the world has lived his whole life without ever being defeated at what they do.

When you see it as being inevitable you are preparing yourself subtly for when it happens. This way you will not be surprised and you will be able to gather yourself quickly and effectively.

See defeat as a learning opportunity

I learned much more from defeat than I ever learned from winning.—*Author unknown*

When asked how he got so good at boxing, Muhammad Ali replied that for three seconds after making every mistake, he thought about it, redid the move, and then moved on. This is smart.

If you see defeat as a learning opportunity, you will grow and change and be able to prepare for the next time you are defeated. If you refuse to learn from it, the only thing that will happen is that you will get upset and probably lose some cash. That's it. If, however, you figure out how it happened, why it happened, and how you can prevent it from happening again, then you will be turning the defeat into something truly meaningful.

See defeat as impermanent

Nothing lasts. Not even defeat. The emotional feelings that come with defeat also do not last. Move on. If you get weighed down by your defeat, you will not be able to move on. If you realize that it is not going to last, however, you will not be as emotionally affected, and you will be prepared to regather as soon as it is over.

See defeat as a mere concept

When you read about great people who have had defeats in their lives, they always seem to view defeat differently from most people. This leads me to believe that defeat is not actually an inherently existing entity. It can be transformed. Defeat is only defeat if you consider it so. If, however, you choose to view defeat in a different light, you will realize that *defeat* is merely a concept, a label, and has no lasting reality to it at all.

Study history's defeats

To learn more ways to deal with defeat, it is a really good idea to look at the major defeats in history. When we study these historical events, we can take away important lessons about what to do and what not to do. You might want to look at some major defeats like that which happens to a country at war, or some more minor defeats, such as what happens to famous people in their careers.

Chapter 17
Change Agent

• • • • • • • • • • • • •

Be the change you want to see in the world.—*Ghandi*

Everyone is a great person, but not everyone has the innate skills to overcome adversity when their expectations are not met or when they are faced with a loss, a failure, or a defeat.

Adversity can be problematic and can lead to anger if the reasons for the adversity are not obvious. Anger is often regarded as negative; American culture teaches us that it's all right to express anxiety, depression, and certain other negative emotions, but not anger. As a result, some people don't understand how to handle anger or how to channel it constructively.

Great people learn skills that allow them to find peace when faced with adversity. Great people acquire coping skills that allow them to understand why a setback is not a defeat, but an opportunity to impart valuable lifelong lessons to those that witness their adversity. Great people do not sit back and witness others being harmed, but will use a case of adversity as an opportunity to test their resolve and to provide a chance to reap a rich harvest of learned experience. Adversity tests one's ability and courage.

Adversity provides opportunities to keep one awake, active, alert, and ready to cope with any situation that arises.

Great people learn to use a diversity of both conscious and unconscious processes to deal with their angry feelings. The three main approaches are:

1. Expressing

2. Suppressing

3. Calming

Great people learn to express their angry feelings in an assertive—not aggressive—manner. Assertive behavior is the healthiest way to express anger. To do this, you have to learn how to make clear what your needs are, and how to get them met, without hurting others. Being assertive doesn't mean being pushy or demanding; it means being respectful of yourself and others.

Adversity does not bring out the best in everyone because it tests our ability to overcome challenge, harshness, and suffering. Great people learn to suppress their anger, and to convert it or redirect it. This happens when you hold in your anger, stop thinking about it, and focus on something positive. The aim is to inhibit or suppress your anger and convert it into more constructive behavior. The danger in this type of response is that if it isn't allowed outward expression, your anger can turn inward—on yourself. Anger turned inward may cause hypertension, high blood pressure, or depression.

Great people also learn that unexpressed anger can create other problems. It can lead to pathological expressions of anger, such as passive-aggressive behavior. It may masquerade as a means to get back at people indirectly, without telling them why, rather than confronting them head-on. Or it may produce a personality trait that seems perpetually cynical and hostile. People who constantly put others down, criticize everything, and make cynical comments haven't learned how to express their anger constructively. Not surprisingly, they aren't likely to have many successful relationships.

Great people learn to calm down internally. This means not just controlling their outward behavior, but also controlling their internal responses, taking steps to lower their heart rate, calm themselves down, and let the feelings subside.

Great people learn to practice appropriate coping skills when faced with adversity. One simple way to avoid adversity is to understand the cause or reason behind the origin of the defeat, failure, or loss. Great people are able to overcome and sustain adversity when given reasons for their defeat, failure, or loss. Knowing the reasons for adversity suggests steps necessary for closure, and to begin the process leading to introspective peace.

Without knowing the reasons for adversity, sufferers are unable to find closure that leads them to peace and resolve. Without reasons, the outcome will more certainly head to a negative adverse effect, possibly an act of violence that could have been prevented in the beginning stages of acceptance and closure.

It is difficult to make a man miserable while he feels worthy of himself and claims kindred to the great God who made him.—*Abraham Lincoln*

Chapter 18
Adversity and Anger

• • • • • • • • • • • •

**Courage is the price that life exacts for granting peace.
The soul that knows it not, knows no release from little
things; knows not the livid loneliness of fear.**
—Amelia Earhart

dversity may cause anger, which may masquerade itself as a fleeting annoyance or as a full-fledged rage. Anger is a natural, adaptive response to adversity or threats. Anger inspires powerful, often aggressive feelings and behaviors, which allow us to fight and to defend ourselves when we are attacked. Anger can also be triggered by memories of traumatic or enraging events that never had closure. A certain amount of anger, therefore, is necessary to survive, but if unattended and allowed to fester, anger can be the most destructive force in anyone's body.

Indirect adversity or conflict can cause intense emotional pain, stress, and anger, especially if those in power recruit others to help fight their battles. This is a common technique used by people who hold the keys to the kingdom. They use power skillfully, requesting or suggesting that their subordinates display indirect conflict toward someone who has been targeted.

It is through this time, that you will find the inner strength to make it better. A person who has never lived through such an experience cannot claim to have gone through the acid test of adversity, which not only brings out the best in human qualities, but makes a person courageous enough to want to fight against the storms in life and elevate to great heights. Through darkest and failed days, one emerges with a richer perspective of emotional human poverty and human deprivation, and thus becomes better equipped, with unshakable self-confidence and character. Self-confidence is the key to great character and the path to great success in life.

When our success is distorted by our failures, we try to find the reasons for those failures, or to understand where we have erred or where the failure really lies. As I wrote in chapter 1, I now reward myself for my failures, because I know my failures will lead to successes. I just have to keep trying.

Adversity gives us a chance to mend our failures for the future. Adversity gives us an opportunity to make something better. Adversity develops a sense of sympathy for others. A person who has never undergone the strains and stresses of adversity cannot understand and appreciate the feelings and emotions of those who may have been placed in unfavorable situations.

Here are some strategies to aid you get through a negative conflict.

1. Engage in physical activities such as deep breathing, yoga, and walking.

2. Think differently about the situation.

3. Solve problems and avoid confrontation.

4. Communicate more effectively; repeat what you thought you heard or what the other person said.

5. Use humor to balance the moment.

6. Change the place where there is a dispute; move if necessary.

Chapter 19
Seven Kinds of People You Need
in Your Corner 6 + 1=7

• • • • • • • • • • • • •

**Courage is resistance to fear, mastery of fear,
not absence of fear. Except a creature be part coward,
it is not a compliment to say it is brave.**
—Mark Twain

When faced with adversity, great people learn to allow their circle of friends' aid in their struggles. Nothing incredible is accomplished alone, and with adversity, no one should go it alone. Everyone needs others, and we all need to help others. With the right people in your corner, you can form a network of connections or a circle of friends to make the seemingly impossible practically inevitable. When faced with defeat, failure, or loss, these seven types of people will provide the little voice in the back of your head that says: *You can do it. You will make it. We will find the solutions, and I am not going to give up on you.*

1. The Instigator

The instigator is someone who pushes you, who makes you think, who motivates you to get up and go, and try, and makes things happen. The instigator keeps you energized and enthusiastic. The instigator is the voice of inspiration, the voice of reason.

2. **The Cheerleader**

The cheerleader is a huge fan, a strong supporter, and a rabid evangelist for you and your work. Work to reward this person, to keep her engaged. The cheerleader is the voice of motivation.

3. **The Doubter**

The doubter is the devil's advocate, the one who asks the hard questions and sees problems before they arise. You need this person's perspective because he is looking out for you, and wants you to be as safe as you are successful. The doubter is the voice of reason.

4. **The Taskmaster**

The taskmaster is the loud and belligerent voice that demands you get things done. This person is the steward of momentum, making sure deadlines are met and goals are reached. The taskmaster is the voice of progress.

5. **The Connector**

The connector helps you find new avenues and new allies. This person breaks through roadblocks and finds ways to make magic happen. You need this person to reach people and places you can't. The connector is the voice of cooperation and community.

6. **The Mentor**

The mentor is your hero, your North Star. This is the person you seek to emulate, your guiding entity, someone whose presence acts as a constant reminder that you, too, can do amazing things. You want to make this person proud. Your North Star is the voice of true authority.

7. You and Only You

You are the only person who knows you the best. Be brave and true to yourself, and in the end, remember those three special people: me, myself and I.

> **It is from numberless diverse acts of courage and belief that human history is shaped. Each time a man stands up for an ideal or acts to improve the lot of others or strikes out against injustice, he sends forth a tiny ripple of hope, and crossing each other from a million different centers of energy and daring those ripples build a current which can sweep down the mightiest walls of oppression and resistance.—*Robert F. Kennedy***

Chapter 20
Second Chances

• • • • • • • • • • • •

In War: Resolution. In Defeat: Defiance.
In Victory: Magnanimity. In Peace: Goodwill.
—*Winston Churchill*

Cultural and societal lessons should and need to include ways to learn how to accept challenges, failure, defeat, and loss in an appropriate way. We can't all be winners, but we should all be given second chances, especially if an outcome results in personal and professional damage that serves no purpose, and only causes direct harm to a person.

The only difference between an opportunity and an obstacle is attitude. Getting a second chance in life is about giving yourself the opportunity to grow beyond your past failures. It's about positively adjusting your attitude toward future possibilities.

However, second chances are not always up to the ones who need them. In many cases, a second chance is not our own decision because the power players hold the keys to the kingdom.

We rarely get things right the first time. Almost every major accomplishment in a person's life starts with a decision to try again—to get up after a failed attempt and give it another shot.

Remember: life is not easy, especially when you plan on achieving something worthwhile. Achieving your dreams can be a lot of work, even the second time around. Be ready for it. So here are a few constructive ideas that might help overcome a failure, loss, or defeat.

- **Let go of the past.**

What's done is done. When life throws us nasty curveballs, it typically doesn't make any sense to us, and our natural emotional reaction might be to get extremely upset and scream obscenities at the top of our lungs. But how does this help our dilemma? Obviously, it doesn't.

The smartest and oftentimes hardest thing we can do in these situations is to be more tempered in our reactions. We want to shout, but need to be wiser and more disciplined than that, to remember that emotional rage only makes matters worse; and to remember that tragedies are rarely as bad as they seem. Even when they are, they give us opportunities to grow stronger.

Every difficult moment in our lives is accompanied by an opportunity for personal growth and creativity. But in order to attain this growth and creativity, we must first learn to let go of the past. We must recognize that difficulties pass like everything else in life. And once they pass, all we're left with are our unique experiences and the resolve to make a better attempt next time.

- **Identify the lesson.**

Everything—everyone you meet and everything you encounter—offers a life lesson. It's all part of the learning experience we call *life*.

Never forget to acknowledge the lesson, especially when things don't go your way. If you don't get a job you wanted or a relationship doesn't work, it only means something better is out there waiting. And the lesson you just learned is the first step toward it.

- **Lose the negative attitude.**

Negative thinking creates negative results. Positive thinking creates positive results.

Every one of the other suggestions in this chapter is irrelevant if your mind is stuck in the gutter. Positive thinking is at the forefront of every great success story. The mind must believe it can do something before it is capable of actually doing it.

- **Accept accountability for your current situation.**

Either you accept accountability for your life or someone else will. And when someone else does it, you'll become a slave to that person's ideas and dreams instead of a pioneer of your own.

You are the only one who can directly control the outcome of your life. And no, it won't always be easy. Every person has a stack of obstacles in front of him. You must take accountability for your situation and overcome these obstacles.

- **Focus on the things you can change.**

Some forces are out of your control. The best thing you can do is do the best with what's in front of you with the resources you have access to.

- First item of a bullet list

- Last item of a bullet list

Wasting your time, talent, and emotional energy on things that are beyond your control is a recipe for frustration, misery, and stagnation. Invest your energy in the things you can change.

- **Eliminate the nonessential.**

First, identify the essential—the things in your life that matter most to you. Then eliminate the fluff. This drastically simplifies things and leaves you with a clean slate—a fresh, solid foundation to build upon without needless interferences. This process works with any aspect of your life: work projects, relationships, general to-do lists, and all the rest.

Remember, you can't accomplish anything if you're trying to accomplish everything. Concentrate on the essential. Get rid of the rest.

- **Be very specific.**

When you set new goals for yourself, try to be as specific as possible. "I want to lose twenty pounds" is a goal you can aim to achieve. "I want to lose weight" is not. Knowing the specific measurements of what you want to achieve is the only way you will ever get to the end result you desire.

- **Concentrate on *doing* instead of *not* doing.**

"Don't think about eating that chocolate donut!" What are you thinking about now? Eating that chocolate donut, right? When you concentrate on not thinking about something, you end up thinking about it.

The same philosophy holds true when it comes to breaking our bad habits. By relentlessly trying not to do something, we end up thinking about it so much that we subconsciously provoke ourselves to cheat—to do the exact thing we are trying not to do.

- **Create a daily routine.**

It's a simple idea: creating a daily routine for yourself can change your life.

The most productive routines, I've found, come at the start and end of the day—of both your workday and your day in general. Therefore, develop a routine for when you wake up, for when you first start working, for when you finish your work, and for the hour or two before you go to sleep.

Doing so will help you start each day on point, and end each day in a way that prepares you for tomorrow. It will help you focus on the important stuff, instead of the distractions that keep popping up. And most importantly, it will help you make steady progress— which is what second chances are all about.

- **Work on it for real.**

The harder you work the luckier you will become. Stop waiting around for things to work out. If you keep doing what you're doing, you'll keep getting what you're getting.

While many of us decide at some point during the course of our lives that we want to answer our calling, only an astute few of us actually work on it. By "working on it," I mean truly devoting oneself to the end result. The rest of us never act on our decision. Or, at best, we pretend to act on it by putting forth an uninspired, half-assed effort.

If you want a real second chance, you've got to be willing to give it all you've got. No slacking off! This means you have to strengthen and maintain your self-control. The best way I've found to do this is to take one small bite of the elephant at a time. Start with just one activity, and make a plan for how you will deal with troubles when they arise. For instance, if you're trying to lose weight, come up with a list of healthy snacks you can eat when you get the craving for snacks. It will be hard in the beginning, but it will get easier. And that's the whole point. As your strength grows, you can take on bigger challenges.

Second Chance Checklist

1. **Turn unproductive regrets into productive regrets.**

Regrets are important in our life to help us self-correct. The key is to recover from and build on the sharp sting of regrets, looking for the lesson to be learned. Take comfort in the fact that these lessons make us wiser.

2. **Take comfort in knowing that regrets help us develop empathy for others.**

How would we ever develop real empathy if we never made a mistake or a wrong turn? It is regrets that keep us in check from being judgmental and arrogant. Thus, we become better people who, in turn, have more compassion and empathy for others.

Empathy is considered to be one of the cornerstones of emotional intelligence.

3. **The more wrong turns you made, the greater the odds that your future choices will be more informed.**

With so many lessons from mistakes or regrets, you will be in better shape moving forward. It can actually make it easier for us to be happier by living in today instead of yesterday.

4. **Ask yourself: Did I do the best I could at the time? Undoubtedly the answer will be yes!**

People generally try their best, even if objectively speaking their best is not healthy. Unhealthy people make unhealthy decisions and behave in unhealthy ways. People do not intentionally make self-defeating decisions. So consider it a noble effort to try your best, even if your best falls short and is misguided.

5. **Moving from regrets is an opportunity to work on the ability to forgive.**

Lack of forgiveness for oneself or others is one of the most common reasons for depression, anxiety, and interpersonal conflict. Thankfully, regrets give you an opportunity to self-correct and to develop the ability to forgive. Strive to be thankful for this golden opportunity to relieve yourself of bitterness and negativity for good!

6. **Use the broken pieces of unrealized dreams and disappointments as stepping stones toward a better future.**

If you see shattered pieces of your life's dreams as stepping stones or as parts of a beautiful life mosaic, you can appreciate those broken remnants. All your disappointments, no matter how small or how large, can be part of something so beautiful that it can be hard to imagine, and can pave the way for building a better tomorrow!

I long to accomplish a great and noble task, but it is my chief duty to accomplish small tasks as if they were great and noble.—*Helen Keller*

Chapter 21
Failure

● ● ● ● ● ● ● ● ● ● ● ● ●

No man can always be right. So, the struggle is to do one's best; to keep the brain and conscience clear; never to be swayed by unworthy motives or inconsequential reason, but to strive to unearth the basic factors involved and then do one's duty.
—*Dwight D. Eisenhower*

Have you ever failed?

History cites examples of people who started from scratch and rose to eminence. Seemingly insurmountable difficulties plagued them in the course of their careers, but they faced them bravely and ultimately refused to be dominated by them. A YouTube video describes the following persons of great prominence with little hope of success, yet, against all odds they raised themselves to distinction in their respective field of work. Life can be full of surprise, and there are many success stories of those who have been rejected or told they were failures and rose to accomplished positions.

Famous Failures

If you never failed, you have never tried anything new. Most of us fear failure. We fear making mistakes and we fear losing, but without failure there is no success. Without mistakes there is no winning. You must fail, you must make mistakes, and you must lose sometimes, but only in preparation for your greatest of glories.

Defeat is never failure unless you allow it to be. Failure is just a learning process, a small detour on your journey to success. If you stop, than defeat is failure, if you persevere, than the defeat is merely a step forward to the path to success

YouTube

Michael Jordan: He was cut from his high school basketball team. He went home, locked himself in his room, and cried.

Albert Einstein: He wasn't able to speak until he was almost four years old, and his teachers said he would never amount to much.

Oprah Winfrey: She was demoted from her job as a news anchor because when they told her she wasn't fit for television.

Lucile Ball: She was dismissed from drama school with a note that said she was wasting her time and that she was too shy to put her best foot forward.

Walt Disney: He was fired from a newspaper for lacking imagination and having no original ideas.

Lionel Messi: He was cut from his team at age eleven after being diagnosed with a growth hormone deficiency that made him smaller in stature than most kids his age.

Steve Jobs: He was devastated and depressed at thirty years of age after being unceremoniously removed from the company he started.

Eminem: He was a high school dropout whose personal struggles with drugs and poverty culminated in an unsuccessful suicide attempt.

Thomas Edison: He had a teacher who told him he was too stupid to learn anything and that he should go into a field where he might succeed by virtue of his pleasant personality.

The Beatles: They were rejected by Decca Records, who told their manager, "We don't like their sound. … They have no future in show business."

Dr. Seuss: His first book was rejected by twenty-seven publishers.

Ulysses S. Grant: A failed solider, farmer, and real-estate agent, at age thirty-eight he went to work for his father as a handyman.

Abraham Lincoln: His fiancée died, he failed in business, he had a nervous breakdown, and he was defeated in eight elections.

Not everyone who's on top today got there with success after success. More often than not, those whom history remembers best were faced with numerous obstacles that forced them to work harder and show more determination than others.

The same can be said for education. Furthering your education with a bachelor's or master's degree can also help do wonders for your success. Next time you're feeling down about your failures in college or in a career, keep these fifty famous people in mind, and remind yourself that sometimes failure is just the first step toward success.

Business Gurus

These businessmen and the companies they founded are today known around the world, but as these stories show, their beginnings weren't always smooth.

Henry Ford: While Ford is known today for his innovative assembly line and American-made cars, he wasn't an instant success. In fact, his early businesses failed and left him broke five times before he founded the successful Ford Motor Company.

R. H. Macy: Most people are familiar with his large department store chain, but Macy didn't always have it easy. Macy started seven failed businesses before finally hitting big with his store in New York City.

F. W. Woolworth: Some may not know this name today, but Woolworth was once one of the biggest names in department stores in the US. Before starting his own business, young Woolworth worked at a dry goods store and was not allowed to wait on customers because his boss said he lacked the sense needed to do so.

Soichiro Honda: The multibillion-dollar business that is Honda began with a series of failures and fortunate turns of luck. Honda was turned down by Toyota Motor Corporation for a job after interviewing for a job as an engineer, leaving him jobless for quite some time. He started making scooters of his own at home, and spurred on by his neighbors, finally started his own business.

Akio Morita: You may not have heard of Morita, but you've

undoubtedly heard of his company, Sony. Sony's first product was a rice cooker that unfortunately didn't cook rice so much as burn it, selling less than a hundred units. This first setback didn't stop Morita and his partners as they pushed forward to create a multibillion-dollar company.

Bill Gates: Gates didn't seem like a shoo-in for success after dropping out of Harvard and starting a failed first business with Microsoft co-founder Paul Allen called Traf-O-Data. While this early idea didn't work, Gates's later work did, creating the global empire that is Microsoft.

Harland David Sanders: Perhaps better known as Colonel Sanders of Kentucky Fried Chicken fame, Sanders had a hard time selling his chicken at first. In fact, his famous secret chicken recipe was rejected 1,009 times before a restaurant accepted it.

Walt Disney: Today Disney rakes in billions from merchandise, movies, and theme parks around the world, but Walt Disney himself had a bit of a rough start. He was fired by a newspaper editor because he lacked imagination and had no good ideas. After that, Disney started a number of businesses that didn't last too long and ended with bankruptcy and failure. He kept plugging along, however, and eventually found a recipe for success that worked.

Scientists and Thinkers

These people are often regarded as some of the greatest minds of all time, but they often had to face great obstacles, the ridicule of their peers, and the animosity of society.

Albert Einstein: Most of us take Einstein's name as synonymous with genius, but he didn't always show such promise. Einstein did not speak until he was four and did not read until he was seven, causing his teachers and parents to think he was mentally handicapped, slow, and antisocial. Eventually he was expelled from school and was refused admittance to the Polytechnic Institute in Zurich. It might have taken him a bit longer, but most people would agree that he caught on pretty well in the end, winning the Nobel Prize and changing the face of modern physics.

Charles Darwin: In his early years, Darwin gave up on having a medical career and was often chastised by his father for being lazy and too dreamy. Darwin himself wrote, "I was considered by all my masters and my father, a very ordinary boy, rather below the common standard of intellect." Perhaps they judged too soon, as Darwin today is well-known for his scientific studies.

Robert Goddard: Today Goddard is hailed for his research and experimentation with liquid-fuel rockets, but during his lifetime his ideas were often rejected and mocked by his scientific peers, who thought they were outrageous and impossible. Today rockets and space travel don't seem farfetched at all, due in part to the work of this scientist who worked against the feelings of the time.

Isaac Newton: Undoubtedly a genius when it came to math, Newton had some failings early on. He never did particularly well in school or when put in charge of running the family farm. He failed miserably—so poorly, in fact, that an uncle took charge and sent him off to Cambridge where he finally blossomed into the scientist we know today.

Socrates: Despite leaving no written records behind, Socrates is regarded as one of the greatest philosophers of the Classical era. Because of his new ideas, in his own time he was called "an immoral corrupter of youth" and was sentenced to death. Socrates didn't let this stop him and kept right on, teaching up until he was forced to poison himself.

Robert Sternberg: This big name in psychology received a *C* in his first college introductory psychology class. His teacher told him that there was already a famous Sternberg in psychology and it was obvious there would not be another. Ouch! Sternberg showed him, however, graduating from Stanford with exceptional distinction in psychology, summa cum laude, and Phi Beta Kappa. He eventually become the President of the American Psychological Association.

Inventors

These inventors changed the face of the modern world, but not without a few failed prototypes along the way.

Thomas Edison: In his early years, teachers told Edison he was too stupid to learn anything. Work was no better, as he was fired from his first two jobs for not being productive enough. Even as an inventor, Edison made a thousand unsuccessful attempts at inventing the light bulb. Of course, all those unsuccessful attempts finally resulted in the design that worked.

Orville and Wilbur Wright: These brothers battled depression and family illness before starting the bicycle shop that would lead them to experimenting with flight. After numerous attempts at creating flying machines, several years of hard work, and tons of failed prototypes, the brothers finally created a plane that could get airborne and stay there.

Public Figures

From politicians to talk show hosts, these figures had a few failures before they came out on top.

Winston Churchill: This Nobel Prize-winning, twice-elected Prime Minster of the United Kingdom wasn't always as well regarded as he is today. Churchill struggled in school and failed his sixth year. After school he faced many years of political failures, as he was defeated in every election for public office until he finally became the Prime Minister at the ripe old age of sixty-two.

Abraham Lincoln: While today he is remembered as one of the greatest leaders of our nation, Lincoln's life wasn't so easy. In his youth he went to war a captain and returned a private. (Private is the lowest rank.) Lincoln didn't stop failing there, however. He started numerous businesses that failed, and was defeated in several runs he made for public office.

Oprah Winfrey: Most people know Oprah as one of the most iconic faces on TV as well as one of the richest and most successful women in the world. Oprah faced a hard road to get to that position, however, enduring a rough and often abusive childhood as well as numerous career setbacks, including being fired from her job as a television reporter because she was "unfit for TV."

Harry S. Truman: This World War I vet, senator, vice president, and eventual president eventually found success in his life, but not without a few missteps along the way. Truman started a store that sold silk shirts and other clothing—seemingly a success at first—only goes bankrupt a few years later.

Dick Cheney: This recent vice president and businessman made his way to the White House but managed to flunk out of Yale University, not once, but twice. Yale graduate and Former President George W. Bush joked with Cheney about this fact, stating, "So now we know—if you graduate from Yale, you become president. If you drop out, you get to be vice president."

Show Biz Types

These faces ought to be familiar from the entertainment industry, but these actors, actresses, and directors saw their fair share of rejection and failure before they made it big.

Jerry Seinfeld: Just about everybody knows who Seinfeld is, but the first time the young comedian walked on stage at a comedy club, he looked out at the audience, froze, and was eventually jeered and booed off of the stage. Seinfeld knew he could do it, so he went back the next night, completed his set to laughter and applause, and the rest is history.

Fred Astaire: In his first screen test, the testing director of MGM noted that Astaire "Can't act. Can't sing. Slightly bald. Can dance a little." Astaire went on to become an incredibly successful actor, singer, and dancer and kept that note in his Beverly Hills home to remind him of where he came from.

Sidney Poitier: After his first audition, Poitier was told by the casting director, "Why don't you stop wasting people's time and go out and become a dishwasher or something?" Poitier vowed to show him that he could make it, going on to win an Oscar and become one of the most highly-regarded actors in the business.

Jeanne Moreau: As a young actress just starting out, this French actress was told by a casting director that she was simply not pretty enough to make it in films. He couldn't have been more wrong, as Moreau went on to star in nearly one hundred films and win numerous awards for her performances.

Charlie Chaplin: It's hard to imagine film without the iconic Charlie Chaplin, but his act was initially rejected by Hollywood studio chiefs because they felt it was a little too nonsensical to ever sell.

Lucille Ball: During her career, Ball had thirteen Emmy nominations and four wins, also earning the Lifetime Achievement Award from the Kennedy Center Honors. Before starring in *I Love Lucy*, Ball was widely regarded as a failed actress and a B movie star. Even her drama instructors didn't feel she could make it, telling her to try another profession. She, of course, proved them all wrong.

Harrison Ford: In his first film, Ford was told by the movie execs that he simply didn't have what it takes to be a star. Today, with numerous hits under his belt, iconic portrayals of characters like Han Solo and Indiana Jones, and a career that stretches decades, Ford can proudly show that he does, in fact, have what it takes.

Marilyn Monroe: While Monroe's star burned out early, she did have a period of great success in her life. Despite a rough upbringing and being told by modeling agents that she should instead consider being a secretary, Monroe became a pinup model and actress who still strikes a chord with people today.

Oliver Stone: This Oscar-winning filmmaker began his first novel while at Yale, a project that eventually caused him to fail out of school. This would turn out to be a poor decision, as the text was rejected by publishers and was not published until 1998, at which time it was not well received. After dropping out of school, Stone moved to Vietnam to teach English, later enlisting in the army and fighting in the war, a battle that earned him two Purple Hearts and helped him find the inspiration for his later work, which often centers on war.

Writers and Artists

We've all heard about starving artists and struggling writers, but these stories show that sometimes all that work really does pay off with success in the long run.

Vincent Van Gogh: During his lifetime, Van Gogh sold only one painting, and this was to a friend and for a very small amount of money. While Van Gogh was never a success during his life, he plugged on with painting, sometimes starving to complete his over eight hundred known works. Today, they bring in hundreds of millions of dollars.

Emily Dickinson: Recluse and poet Emily Dickinson is a commonly read and loved writer. Yet in her lifetime she was all but ignored, having fewer than a dozen poems published out of her almost 1,800 completed works.

Theodor Seuss Giesel: Today nearly every child has read *The Cat in the Hat* or *Green Eggs and Ham*, yet twenty-seven different publishers rejected Dr. Seuss's first book *To Think That I Saw It on Mulberry Street.*

Charles Schulz: The *Peanuts* comic strip Schulz created has had enduring fame, yet this cartoonist had every cartoon he submitted rejected by his high school yearbook staff. Even after high school Schulz didn't have it easy, applying and being rejected for a position working with Walt Disney.

Steven Spielberg: While today Spielberg's name is synonymous with big-budget movies, he was rejected from the University of Southern California School of Theater, Film, and Television three times. He eventually attended school at another location, only to drop out to become a director before finishing. Thirty-five years after starting his degree, in 2002, Spielberg returned to school to finally complete his work and earn his BA.

Stephen King: The first book by this author, the iconic thriller *Carrie,* received thirty rejections. King finally gave up and threw it in the trash. His wife fished it out and encouraged him to resubmit it, and the rest is history today, with countless books published, King has the distinction of being one of the best-selling authors of all time.

Zane Grey: Incredibly popular in the early twentieth century, this adventure book writer began his career as a dentist, something he quickly began to hate. So he began to write, only to see rejection after rejection for his works, being told eventually that he had no business being a writer and should give up. It took him years, but at age forty Zane finally got his first work published. In the end he authored almost ninety books, selling over fifty million copies worldwide.

J. K. Rowling: Ms. Rowling may be rolling in a lot of Harry Potter dough today, but before she published the series of novels, she was nearly penniless, severely depressed, divorced, and trying to raise a child on her own while attending school and writing a novel. Rowling went from depending on welfare for survival to being one of the richest women in the world in a span of only five years through her hard work and determination.

Claude Monet: Today Monet's work sells for millions of dollars and hangs in some of the most prestigious institutions in the world. Yet during his own time, it was mocked and rejected by the artistic elite, the Paris Salon. Monet kept at his impressionist style, which caught on, and in many ways was a starting point for some major changes to art that ushered in the modern era.

Jack London: This well-known American author wasn't always such a success. While he would go on to publish popular novels like *White Fang* and *The Call of the Wild*, his first story received six hundred rejection slips before finally being accepted.

Louisa May Alcott: Most people are familiar with Alcott's most famous work, *Little Women*. Yet Alcott faced a bit of a battle to get her work out there and was encouraged to find work as a servant by her family to make ends meet. It was her letters back home during her experience as a nurse in the Civil War that gave her the first big break she needed.

Musicians

While their music is some of the best selling, best loved and most popular around the world today, these musicians show that it takes a whole lot of determination to achieve success.

Wolfgang Amadeus Mozart: Mozart began composing at the age of five, writing over six hundred pieces of music that today are lauded as some of the best ever created. Yet during his lifetime, Mozart didn't have such an easy time, and was often restless, leading to his dismissal from a position as a court musician in Salzburg. He struggled to keep the support of the aristocracy and died with little to his name.

Elvis Presley: As one of the best-selling artists of all time, Elvis has become a household name even years after his death. But back in 1954, Elvis was still a nobody, and Jimmy Denny, manager of the Grand Ole Pry, fired Elvis Presley after just one performance telling him, "You isn't goin' nowhere, son. You ought to go back to drivin' a truck."

Igor Stravinsky: In 1913, when Stravinsky debuted his now famous *Rite of Spring*, audiences rioted, running the composer out of town. Yet it was this very work that changed the way composers in the twentieth century thought about music and cemented Stravinsky's place in musical history.

The Beatles: Few people can deny the lasting power of this super group, still popular with listeners around the world today. Yet when they were just starting out, a recording company told them no. They were told: "we don't like their sound, and guitar music is on the way out," two things the rest of the world couldn't have disagreed with more.

Ludwig van Beethoven: In his formative years, young Beethoven was incredibly awkward on the violin, and was often so busy working on his own compositions that he neglected to practice. Despite his love of composing, his teachers felt he was hopeless at it and would never succeed with the violin or in composing. Beethoven kept plugging along, however, and composed some of the best-loved symphonies of all time–five of them while he was completely deaf.

Athletes

While some athletes rocket to fame, others endure a path fraught with a little more adversity, like those listed here.

A Wrongful Criminal Conviction

Michael Jordan: Most people wouldn't believe that a man often lauded as the best basketball player of all time was actually cut from his high school basketball team. Luckily, Jordan didn't let this setback stop him from playing the game. He has stated, "I have missed more than 9,000 shots in my career. I have lost almost three hundred games. On twenty-six occasions I have been entrusted to take the game-winning shot, and I missed. I have failed over and over and over again in my life. And that is why I succeed."

Stan Smith: This tennis player was rejected from being even a lowly ball boy for a Davis Cup tennis match because event organizers felt he was too clumsy and uncoordinated. Smith went on to prove them wrong, showcasing his not-so-clumsy skills by winning Wimbledon, the US Open, and eight Davis Cups.

Babe Ruth: You probably know Babe Ruth because of his home run record (714 during his career), but along with all those home runs came a pretty hefty number of strikeouts as well (1,330 in all). In fact, for decades he held the record for strikeouts. When asked about this he simply said, "Every strike brings me closer to the next home run."

Tom Landry: As the coach of the Dallas Cowboys, Landry brought the team two Super Bowl victories, won five NFC Championship victories, and holds the record for the most career wins. He also has the distinction of having one of the worst first seasons on record, winning no games, then winning five or fewer over the next four seasons.

Chapter 22
Conclusion

• • • • • • • • • • • • •

Honesty is the first chapter in the Book of Wisdom.
—Thomas Jefferson

A *lesson that everyone needs to* understand is that some people, because of the selfish reasons of others, have been falsely accused of wrongdoing, resulting in malicious prosecution, judicial injustice, and impropriety. Prosecutors prosecute for the sake of prosecution, and make errors of one kind or another, wrongfully accusing and wrongfully convicting an innocent person of a crime which he or she did not commit. This conviction leaves the innocent person languishing, resulting in loss of liberty, civil rights, productive lifestyle, financial and personal ruin, mental anguish, social condemnation, and personal and family embarrassment for the remainder of their lives.

The guarantee of equal protection cannot mean one thing when applied to one person and something else when applied to another. If both are not accorded the same protection, then it is not equal.
—Lewis F. Powell, Jr.

Curriculum Vitae
Anne Boston Parish

• • • • • • • • • • • • •

Education

Marymount University, Doctor of Nursing (Candidate), 2011

Marymount University, Post—MSN FNP Certificate (Summa cum laude), 1995

Marymount University, MSN, 1989

Marymount University, BSN, 1988

Marymount College of Virginia, AAS, 1972

University of Virginia, Sorensen Institute for Political Leadership (Candidate), 2008

Marymount University Honor Society

Sigma Theta Tau National Nursing Honor Society

Delta Sigma Theta National Honor Society

Professional Awards and Honors

Flora Krause Casey Public Health Award, 2010

Alexandria Commission of Public Health and the City of Alexandria Public Health

Marymount University, Alumni Achievement Award, 2008

American Academy of Nursing, *Raising the Voice*: Edge Runner Award, 2008

ABC News WJLA, Toyota Tribute to Working Women Award, 2004

Small Business of the Year, Chamber of Commerce, 2002

Washingtonian of the Year, 2002

Alexandria Commission of Women, Rising Star Award, 2002

Soroptimist International America's Women of Distinction, 2002

Alumni Board

Marymount University, 2009–2011

Professional Activities

American Academy of Nurse Practitioners, Certified Family Nurse Practitioner

American Nurses Association, Certified Family Nurse Practitioner

RN State Board affiliations: Virginia (Tri-State) and California

FNP State Board privileges: Virginia, Maryland, Washington DC, California, South Carolina

Virginia Prescriptive Authority, Consultant, 2005

On-site marketing and community outreach consultation for Solera

Capital, which owns and operates The Little Clinic in the Southeast and Midwest locations of the United States. The sessions were provided to the CEO, vice president, and the regional directors to provide an understanding of the building blocks in a business from its early stages to the creation of a clinic in the community.

Publications

Parish, A. "ADVANCE for Nurse Practitioners: Serving the Uninsured". 2008.

Parish, A. "Confronting America's Health Care Crisis: Establishing A Clinic for the Medically Uninsured". Author House, 2008.

Parish, A. "Clinical Pearls: Fecal Lubricant". Clinician Reviews, 1997.

Parish, A. "A Snapshot of Nursing Education to Come". Nursing Spectrum, 1994.

Parish, A. "It Only Hurts When I Don't Laugh". American Journal of Nursing, 1994.

Parish, A. "Critical Care RN". Nursing Spectrum, 1994.

Parish, A. "Local Nurse Executives, Nurse Educators Meet with Nurse Recruiters". Nursing Spectrum, 1992.

Parish, A. "Remembering NCLEX". Nursing Spectrum, 1992.

Parish, A. "The School Nurse in Alexandria". 1989.

Clinical Masters Thesis

Research proposal: "The Effect of Family Life Educational Program on Adolescent Pregnancy"

Business Plan: "The On-Site Implementation of a 24-Hour Hospital Child Care Facility"

Clinical Preceptor, 1990–Present

Jacksonville University

Georgetown University

Quinnipiac University

University of Washington

Ball State University

George Washington University, George Mason University

Howard University

Marymount University

University of Virginia

Northern Virginia Community College

Columbia Union College

Full-Time Experience

Queen Street Clinic, PLC, 2001–October 31, 2011

Family Practice for the Medically Uninsured

Owner, Founder, Family Nurse Practitioner, sole medical provider

Biography
Anne Boston Parish

● ● ● ● ● ● ● ● ● ● ● ●

Anne Boston Parish is a family nurse practitioner who resides in Coronado, California. Anne is a graduate of Marymount University in Arlington, Virginia. After raising her children, she used her personal funds to build a clinic for the medically uninsured. Anne has made a considerable contribution to her community for the medically uninsured. She was named in 2002 as a Washingtonian Award recipient. Anne has earned the following degrees:

- Associate Degree in Applied Science, 1972

- Bachelor of Science in Nursing, 1988

- Masters of Science in Nursing, 1989

- Post-Masters Certificate, Family Nurse Practitioner, 1995

- Doctor of Nursing Practice (Candidate), 2011

Anne has been featured in local and national newspapers, as well as in nursing journals, including the following:

- *The Washington Post*

- *Old Town Crier*

- *Alexandria Gazette Packet and The Alexandria Journal*

- *The Alexandria Chamber of Commerce, Chamber Currents*

- *Nursing Spectrum*

- *Nurse Practitioner World News*

- *Advance for Nurses and the American Journal of Nursing*

- *MU Today, The Magazine for Marymount University*

- *Alexandria Times*

- *Del Ray Sun*

Washington, DC's ABC affiliate, Channel 7 News and Toyota honored her by presenting her with a Tribute to the Working Women Award in 2004. CNN and ABC affiliate Channel 7 News in Washington, DC, have also interviewed her. Both Anne and the clinic have received much praise from both her peers and various organizations. The Queen Street Clinic was featured in a DVD for the annual conference of the American Academy of Nurse Practitioners in July 2005. Additionally, Anne has consulted for a number of organizations, including a teleconference with VHA in Irving, Texas, to implement a community-based clinic for the medically uninsured, and a national consumer-focused healthcare company that was building walk-in clinics in supermarkets. She is on the faculty of local universities and has been published in various nursing journals.

In 2007 Anne was nominated to receive a Living Legend Award

for the difference she has made in the Alexandria Community. The Queen Street Clinic is able to provide health care to those less fortunate and who are medically uninsured. In addition to working as the sole medical provider at the Queen Street Clinic, Anne is available for consultation either for long-term projects or short-term profiles.

In 2008 one of her proudest achievements was the publication of her first book: *Confronting America's Health Care Crisis: Establishing a Clinic for the Medically Uninsured*. Most recently Anne was acknowledged by the American Academy of Nursing (AAN) for her efforts in the delivery of health care. Anne's unique delivery of health care and the Queen Street Clinic saved the city of Alexandria $10.6 million in the seven years since she opened the clinic door. Queen Street Clinic is now included in the Raise the Voice Campaign and was presented the accolade of an Edge Runner Profile.

In 2008 Anne received Marymount's Alumni Achievement Award, and in 2011 the City of Alexandria presented her the Flora Krause Casey Public Health Award, the highest public health service award presented for the delivery of public health care for the less fortunate or those without medical insurance.

Since Anne has opened the Queen Street Clinic she has had over 23,000 patient visits for family practice medicine, and her follow-up rate is 60 percent.